Clapham Junction was originally a country crossroads. When the railway arrived in 1839 only a signal box was to be found there. In 1863, however, the London, Brighton & South Coast Railway opened a station, and there was rapid development as a commuter centre. At one time Clapham was the busiest railway junction in the world, with 2500 trains passing through each day. In this photograph, taken in August 1889, station-master Carne sits surrounded by his staff. Their formal pose is broken only by the porter in the rear rank, whose crossed leg, and thumb in waistcoat, seem almost defiant.

THE VICTORIAN RAILWAY WORKER

Trevor May

Shi   s

D0774070

Contents

Front cover: *The driver of 1852: an engraving by J. Harris after a painting by H. Alken, published by Fores of 41 Piccadilly, London, 26th May 1852.*

ACKNOWLEDGEMENTS
The cover illustration is reproduced by courtesy of the National Railway Museum and the Science and Society Picture Library. Other illustrations are acknowledged as follows: Brunel University Library, pages 4 (top right), 13, 21 (both), 22 (top), 24 (top), 27 (both), 28, 30 (bottom), 31, 32; Corinium Museum, Cirencester, page 19 (top); Dover Pictorial Archive, page 14 (bottom right); Leicestershire Museums Arts and Records Service, pages 9 (top), 14 (top), 19 (upper centre); London Borough of Harrow Library Service, page 22 (centre); National Railway Museum, York, pages 1, 3, 4 (top left), 5 (top), 18 (bottom), 20, 24 (bottom), 25 (top); author's collection, pages 4 (bottom), 5 (bottom), 6, 7, 8, 10 (top and centre), 12, 14 (bottom left), 15 (left), 16 (both), 18 (top), 19 (bottom centre), 22 (bottom), 25 (bottom), 26 (both), 29 (both).

British Library Cataloguing in Publication Data: May, Trevor. The Victorian railway worker. – (A Shire album) 1. Railroads – Great Britain – Employees – History – 19th century I. Title 385'. 0941'09034 ISBN 0 7478 0451 6.

Published in 2000 by Shire Publications Ltd, Cromwell House, Church Street, Princes Risborough, Buckinghamshire HP27 9AA, UK. (Website: www.shirebooks.co.uk)
Copyright © 2000 by Trevor May. First published 2000. Shire Album 351. ISBN 0 7478 0451 6.
Trevor May is hereby identified as the author of this work in accordance with Section 77 of the Copyright, Designs and Patents Act 1988.
Printed in Great Britain by CIT Printing Services Ltd, Press Buildings, Merlins Bridge, Haverfordwest, Pembrokeshire SA61 1XF.

The scale and range of railway employment

Within a generation of the start of the Railway Age, railways had climbed high on the table of occupations. By 1850, when around 60,000 people were directly employed by railway companies, railway service had reached thirty-third place. By 1870 it had reached sixth, and accounted for 3 per cent of the national workforce. Over 250,000 people worked for railway companies by 1875, when there were more than 49,000 porters, over 19,000 drivers and foremen, nearly 13,000 signalmen, and around 5000 station-masters. Thirty years later roughly 600,000 people worked for British railway companies. Rather more than half represented the managerial and operational staff of the lines. About 200,000, or one third of the total, were engaged on the maintenance and renewal of the rolling-stock and permanent-way. The remaining 80,000 or so looked after what a contemporary writer described as the 'side shows': hotels and refreshment rooms, docks, steamships, railway-owned canals, and a host of activities necessary to keep these vast enterprises ticking over.

In 1905 the London & North Western Railway (with 1946 miles, 3132 km, of track, the second longest after the Great Western) employed 82,835 people. These they classified into no fewer than 801 categories. There were hookers-on and slippers, chair-gaugers and wheel-tappers, lock-attendants and lampmen, firemen (either to maintain fires on locomotives or to extinguish fires in buildings) and fire-droppers, gas-fitters and gardeners, horse-keepers and timekeepers.

Not all railway employees were men. Women were employed not only as barmaids and waitresses in refreshment rooms, or maids in hotels, but as laundry workers,

Many railway employees worked in what might be considered 'support services'. These proud firemen, photographed with their horse-drawn 'steamer' in February 1910, were employed by the Midland Railway at its Derby works. Several companies had their own photographic department. The Midland opened one at Derby in 1882, the first photographer being Thomas Scotton, formerly a painter's labourer.

Two very different 'railwaymen'. Thomas Lewis (left) was a guard on the Wrexham and Ellesmere line of the Cambrian Railway and was photographed around 1896. Captain J. Chilver (right) was a seaman. In 1912 he commanded the Great Eastern Railway's Royal Mail turbine steamer, the 'St Petersburg', and was commodore of that company's fleet. This photograph appeared in the 'Great Eastern Railway Magazine'.

telegraph clerks, and in the manufacture of sacks and tarpaulins. Nor were they all adults. For example, boys were employed to sort all the collected tickets (learning some railway geography at the same time), a task which, by the start of the twentieth century, was given by some companies to girls, who were considered more deft and more methodical.

The railway companies have been likened to vast armies. Many of the early

George Cruikshank produced this engraving in 1847. The coachman complains that their 'whole consarn has been regularly smashed by them Railway chaps'. It is true that the long-distance coaches were quickly forced from the roads, but the railways actually fostered shorter-distance road travel: people and goods had to be brought to and from the stations. Some of this work was carried out by the railway companies themselves, although a large part remained in the hands of contractors or private individuals.

4

Not everyone working at a railway station was a company employee. This young man, in his tweed suit and uniform cap, is a newsboy for W. H. Smith. Smith won an exclusive contract with the London & North Western Railway in 1848. By 1905, when this photograph was taken at Holyhead station, the empire had been extended to many other railway companies. In 1851 W. H. Smith had 35 bookstalls. By 1902 there were 777, with an additional 463 'sub-stalls'.

personnel were in fact drawn from the army and navy, the only other organisations similar in scale. Most workers wore uniform, they 'reported for duty' and were subjected to a discipline only a little less harsh than that of soldiers and sailors. Regulations adopted in 1840 and 1842 provided that a worker who broke the company rules could be brought before the magistrates and, if found guilty, imprisoned for up to two months. Dismissal could be sudden, and in the year ending 31st July 1841 the Great Western Railway threw out 79 of its total labour force of 700.

There were many workers whose livelihood depended on the railways although they were not directly employed by the companies. There were all those who worked on the station bookstalls of W. H. Smith in England and Wales, and John Menzies in Scotland. There were those who worked for contractors supplying uniform clothing as well as a host of railway paraphernalia. And there were other transport workers, such as jobmasters, cab drivers and omnibus or tram workers, who carried a stream of passengers to and from the stations.

The railway companies spawned a host of other enterprises. George Bradshaw, a Manchester Quaker, started to produce his timetables in 1839. He had no serious competitors, and 'Bradshaw' continued to be published for 120 years. The same firm published a 'Railway Manual and Shareholders' Guide', a boon for investors as well as an opportunity for private manufacturers of railway equipment to advertise their wares. The manufacture of signals was largely in the hands of five firms up to the 1860s, the Midland Railway standing almost alone as a manufacturer of its own equipment. When considering 'railway work', such private enterprise must also be reckoned with.

The men who built the railways

When the Stockton & Darlington Railway opened its line in 1825 comparatively little interest was aroused outside its immediate locality. In the next county, the *Yorkshire Gazette* devoted eight lines to the opening ceremony. Railways were not unknown on Tyneside, which already possessed 225 miles (362 km) of industrial track. But a new era was about to dawn. By 1852, 7500 miles (12,000 km) of public railway had been opened; by 1912 the total mileage exceeded 23,000 (37,000 km). Although much of the construction occurred during the 'railway booms' of 1836–7 and 1845–8, railway building was a continuous process, the last main line being the Great Central Railway, built from Nottingham to London between 1894 and 1899. Throughout the nineteenth century, therefore, there was permanent (though fluctuating) demand for railway engineers, contractors, labourers and building workers of all descriptions.

The 'generals' of these vast landscape-changing armies were the engineers. The skills required were manifold, and in the early railway era – when the profession of engineering was itself in its infancy – engineers were drawn from a variety of backgrounds. They included former officers of the Royal Engineers, mining surveyors, mechanical engineers and architects. It was their responsibility to arrange for the survey of the route and to argue its merits before a parliamentary committee. If they were successful there, then it fell to them to arrange the actual contracts for construction and to see that the work proceeded satisfactorily. These tasks were demanding, both mentally and physically: Robert Stephenson is alleged to have walked the whole length of the line between London and Birmingham upwards of twenty times during its construction.

When a route had been selected, it had to be surveyed. This was undertaken with the simplest of equipment: a theodolite, a graduated staff and the surveyor's chain, which measured 22 yards (about 20 metres), the distance between the wickets of a cricket pitch. Experienced surveyors were able to estimate to within a fraction of an inch by eye. However, the comparative simplicity of the process of surveying was

A landowner cocks a snook at a railway surveyor. 'Why, if he hasn't put up a table-cloth' bemoans the surveyor at his 'dumpy level' (theodolite). In reality, clashes between landowners and survey parties often ended in violence. (Cartoon from 'Punch's Almanack for 1846'.)

Robert Stephenson (1803–59) was perhaps the greatest of the railway engineers. He was certainly the first engineering millionaire and when he died in 1859 was buried in Westminster Abbey. The great engineers, like Stephenson and Brunel, became folk heroes.

balanced by the ingenuity needed to outwit landowners who were often anxious to prevent the work being carried out. One clergyman, who owned land along the proposed route of the London & Birmingham Railway, used every expedient possible to prevent his land being surveyed. Not to be outdone, the surveyors waited in readiness one Sunday and nipped on to the land to complete their work while their reverend opponent was delivering his sermon.

Not all engineers were as noteworthy as George and Robert Stephenson, Isambard Kingdom Brunel or Joseph Locke. Nor were all contractors – the men who undertook the actual construction of the railways – of the calibre of Samuel Morton Peto or Thomas Brassey. Men such as these were like medieval barons heading vast armies which had to be kept employed lest they became dispersed. They were thus constantly on the lookout for fresh work, wherever it might take them. In a working life of 35 years, Thomas Brassey undertook 170 contracts, covering 8000 miles (13,000 km) of railway. At one point he had simultaneous contracts for railways and docks in five continents, while, with the exception of Albania, Finland and Greece, every country in Europe had a specimen of his handiwork.

Generally speaking, railway engineers preferred to work with large contractors, who were considered more experienced and better resourced. But, especially at times of peak construction, there simply were not enough of them to go round. As a result, much of the work of railway building was in the hands of men of much more limited means. The railway engineer F. R. Conder suggested that, in addition to London builders, 'Yorkshire masons, Birmingham bricklayers, miners, lime-burners, and quarry owners, often united the business of a builder with their own' and were ready to move into the speculative business of railway construction.

Contracts had to be tendered for. The complete line would generally be broken into sections of an estimated value of between £20,000 and £50,000. Thus, contracts

Never take a picture at face value. This illustration from 'Punch' has, in the past, been used as 'a contemporary illustration of a navvy'. Indeed, it is such, but in rather special circumstances. Not all railway navvies marched around with cutlasses! In 1854, during the Crimean War, it was taking longer to transport supplies from the harbour at Sebastopol to the front lines than it was to ship them from Britain to the Crimea. A group of contractors offered to construct a railway at cost price and to do so recruited a body of navvies who were sent out as a civilian Civil Engineer Corps. This proved a success, and it is one of these navvies prepared for war service who is depicted here.

for the London & Birmingham Railway's line, for example, at a total length of 112 miles (180 km), were originally given to 21 individual contractors and partnerships. The contract would lay down in minute detail the work which was to be undertaken, the materials and methods to be used and, in some cases, the manner in which workers were to be paid. Contractors were sometimes accused of exploiting their construction workers – the navvies. Conder estimated that the return to the contractor on a contract for work might be between 8 and 12 per cent, but that between 30 and 40 per cent was to be made from 'tommy-shops' – company stores set up by the contractor to provide the men with provisions. Most contractors were not crooks, however, simply men living on a knife edge, and the risk of failure was high. Ralph Lawson, a contractor to the Bishop Auckland & Weardale Railway (incorporated 1837), wrote pleadingly to the company:

> The men is coming on me for all there wages and as there is a parte cash in hand for work done since it was measured to be payed on Saderday first I hope that you will take it in concideration so that the men may get there wages for they threaten to Distress me at the justice meeting i was told to pay half of the wages and i have and they are not content.

Lawson was clearly in dread of his navvies. As an occupational group they are easy to stereotype. Even contemporary accounts swung between the devilish and the heroic. Peter Lecount was a former naval officer who found employment as an engineer with the London & Birmingham Railway. In 1839 he wrote of navvies:

> [Having] all the daring recklessness of the Smuggler, without any of his redeeming qualities, their ferocious behaviour can only be equalled by the brutality of their language. It may truly be said, their hand is against every man, and before they have been long located, every man's hand is against them.

F. S. Williams, a Congregational minister and author of *Our Iron Roads*, one of the earliest and best-selling popular accounts of the railways, took an altogether more charitable view:

> As they toil they are the embodiment of physical force in its fullest development of concentrated energy. No man stops to lean for breath on the head of that pickaxe he wields so strenuously. . . . The navvies, bare-throated, their massive torsos covered but by the shirt, their strong, lissom loins lightly girt, and the muscles showing out on their shapely legs through the tight, short breeches, and the ribbed stockings that surmount the ankle-jacks, are the perfection of animal vigour. Finer men I never saw, and never hope to see. . . . Their countenances are manly and ingenuous. . . . A 'waster' among such men would stand ignominiously confessed before the morning's work were half done.

The truth lies somewhere in the middle. Although riotous and drunken behaviour was not unknown, the navvy was probably not the social pariah he is sometimes painted as. Most railway navvies lived in permanent buildings, often as lodgers with local people. They were generally dependent on the host community for food and accommodation. Indeed, many came from the areas through which a line passed.

They were a far from homogeneous group, and the pattern was not entirely dissimilar to that on the canals, in the construction of which the 'navigators' have their origin. There was a migratory element of 'true' navvies, with skills acquired and honed on a succession of projects. These were the men who undertook the dangerous 'barrow-runs', and who handled explosives (often used to blast intractable clay as well as rock). There were Irishmen who had originally arrived to assist with

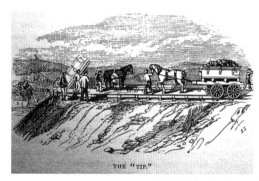

THE "TIP."

Left and below: A tip-truck and horse of a type that was used throughout the period of railway-building. Track would be laid to the end of an embankment under construction and a balk of timber would be fixed across. The horseman would trot the horse towards this buffer, release it from the wagon and give a signal, to which the well-trained horse responded by leaping to one side. The truck, being hinged at the front, shot out its load when the buffer was struck. The horse was then reharnessed so that another load could be collected. (Engraving from F. S. Williams, 'Our Iron Roads', third edition, 1883. Photograph from Charles H. Grinling, 'The Ways of Our Railways', 1905.)

Left: *Vast quantities of bricks were used in railway construction. In the Kilsby tunnel of the London & Birmingham Railway, 36 million bricks were laid, sufficient, it was claimed, 'to make a good footpath from London to Aberdeen (missing the Forth) a yard broad'. With the early railways, at least, temporary brickworks would often be set up along the line. They must have resembled this brickfield photographed at the reconstructed eighteenth-century township of Williamsburg, Virginia. Bricklayers were in much demand and they often travelled around in groups.*

Right: *Gangers and platelayers had the task of maintaining the track once laid. In the 1880s the Great Northern Railway had a thousand platelayers on the line between London and Edinburgh, at wages of between £1 and £1 10s a week. They were out in all weathers repairing the track and had the additional task of laying fog signals when required. Not surprisingly, they had the highest accident rate of all railwaymen. Working methods had hardly changed up to the time this cigarette card was issued between the wars.*

harvest work. The largest concentration of Irish navvies was on lines built in the north of England and the West Midlands, but their numbers fell off later. Then there were local men – often agricultural workers attracted by higher rates of pay. In Northamptonshire in the mid 1830s, for example, a farm labourer might earn 9s or 10s a week, while the railway rate was between 3s and 5s *a day*. To make such a move, if only on a temporary basis, must have been an attractive proposition, although it was not one open to a man who lived in a farmer's tied cottage. Nevertheless, the local contribution to the labour force is evident from the fact that in the south-west of England (where there was little alternative employment to agriculture) between 30 and 40 per cent of the labourers on some lines were born within 10 miles (16 km) of their workplace.

The number of navvies at work on a particular stretch of line also varied. Partly this was a matter of terrain, with twice as many men per mile cutting lines through the Pennines than were needed on the flat land of East Anglia. Also, it depended on urgency, and the importance of the line. The Leeds & Thirsk Railway employed over

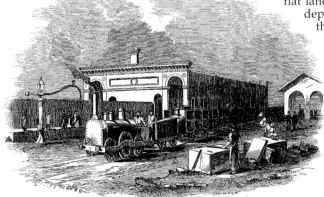

The construction of a railway required the services of every kind of building craftsman, as well as the earth-moving navvies. Here, masons cut stone for the recently opened Cambridge station on the Eastern Counties Railway. (Engraving from the 'Illustrated London News', 2nd August 1845.)

This engraving from the 'Illustrated London News' of 24th March 1849 shows the fitting shop of the Grand Junction Railway at Crewe. As well as eleven planing-machines, 36 shaping and slotting machines and 30 lathes (all steam-powered) there were five sets of benches running nearly the whole 330 foot length of the building. Here, fitters (or 'vice-men') used rasp, file, hammer and other hand tools to fashion the five thousand or so parts which made up an engine. The boy in the illustration reminds us that children were employed at the works, one task being the sorting of iron and brass shavings with a magnet prior to the waste being returned to the foundry.

7000 men at the height of construction, or 185 per mile. On the other hand, the Eden Valley line, which meandered through Cumbria, had about 650 men, spread out at an average of only 30 per mile. Altogether, 200,000 men were involved in construction at the height of the railway mania in 1846. This 'army' can be compared with the 160,000 men who, at that time, constituted the armed forces proper.

Peter Lecount may have had a low opinion of the morals of navvies, but he had a high regard for their capacity to work. Lecount, like many men of his day, loved statistics, especially if they involved vast amounts and could be made visual through some analogy. Thus, he calculated that the earth removed for the construction of the line between London and Birmingham would be sufficient to make a path a foot high and a yard broad around the equator. Questionable though his statistical methods may have been, there can be no doubting that the landscape of Britain was transformed by manual effort, largely unaided by machinery. The contractor Thomas Brassey estimated that an experienced navvy could shift about 16 cubic yards (12.23 cubic metres) of earth and stone in a day, and throw it into a wagon. Visualise a trench a yard deep, a yard across and 16 yards long (915 mm by 915 mm by 14.64 metres) and one can get a sense of the effort expended. The work was hazardous as well as arduous. Edwin Chadwick once shocked a commission of enquiry by pointing out that casualties in the construction of the Woodhead Tunnel amounted to 32 killed and 140 wounded. At 3 per cent of the number employed, the death rate, he concluded, was higher than in the four battles of Talavera, Salamanca, Vittoria and Waterloo.

Included amongst the workers who built the railways were those who manufactured the locomotives and rolling-stock, and those who subsequently maintained them. The railway companies represented substantial manufacturing industries, employing all kinds of industrial worker. Some even produced the raw materials. The London & North Western, for example, had its own steel works,

STEAM FORGING.

BOILER HOUSE.

EXPANDING TIRE.

HEATING WHEEL.

The Great Western Railway works at Swindon, from the 'Illustrated Exhibitor and Magazine of Art', 1852. Engravings such as this give little sense of the noise and bustle of railway workshops. By the mid 1860s the works employed around 1700, rising to a peak of over 14,000 after the First World War. Although in 1852 there were two Nasmyth steam hammers for the heaviest work (one of which is shown here), there were 176 smith's hearths. Blacksmiths, working by hand, continued to play a crucial role throughout the Victorian and Edwardian periods. Alfred Williams, who was a forgehand and hammerman at the works between 1892 and 1914, wrote, 'You see the workmen standing or stooping, pulling, tugging, heaving, dragging to and fro, or staggering about as though they were intoxicated. . . It is a weird living picture, stern and realistic, such as no painter could faithfully reproduce.'

which produced 76,000 tons of steel a year at the beginning of the twentieth century. As well as producing their own locomotives, the larger companies manufactured all manner of railway material. At Crewe, it was said in the 1880s that nothing was imported in manufactured shape other than copper tubes for locomotive boilers. The growth of the Crewe works was phenomenal. In 1843 they covered 2^1/$_2$ acres (just over one hectare) and employed 161 hands; by 1886 they had expanded to 140 acres (56.66 ha) and employed 6000. By the mid 1890s, when the population of the town was around 29,000, over 7000 people earned a living at the works, which had become the largest of their kind in the United Kingdom. At the beginning of the twentieth century, Crewe turned out forty sets of signals and 6000 yards (5500 metres) of point-rodding each month, in addition to the 200 new locomotives built and the 3000 working engines maintained each year. Two men were even employed in the carpentry shop to make artificial limbs, which the company undertook to supply to employees who had lost them in the line of duty!

The men who ran the railways

Railway workers showed a loyalty to their company in the same way that a soldier owed loyalty to his regiment. Each was likely to wear a uniform and each was subject to the strictest discipline. We should not conclude, however, that railwaymen had much fellow-feeling for employees in other grades, or that they knew a great deal about their work. In *Men and Rails*, published in 1913, Rowland Kenney (himself a railwayman) wrote that 'A goods porter may know no more about the engine drivers than the man in the street'. The goods and the passenger sides of railway operation were kept quite distinct and there was a well-defined hierarchy of grades and classifications. Footplatemen tended to look down on 'station men' and 'desk men' as having nothing to do with actually running the trains on the tracks. Such rivalries were not discouraged for, by pursuing a policy of 'divide and rule', the more effective organisation of the workers into trade unions was made more difficult. Grading also provided an incentive, encouraging men to work hard, behave deferentially and hope for transfer to a better-paid job.

There were well-defined routes to certain grades, none more so than that to engine-driver. The first step was to become an engine cleaner. Michael Reynolds, in *Engine-Driving Life* (1881), wrote:

> It takes ten hours at least to clean an engine. It requires no small amount of courage, perseverance, and endurance to clean an engine regularly all the year round, especially when icicles hang by the tender feed-pipe, and the wind whistles shrilly under the shed door.

During the years he was thus employed, he would be taught the duties of a fireman. He would also learn the skills of firing economically, for each week firemen were required to fill in 'coal sheets', a rank order of which was stuck up in the running shed for all to see. At the age of eighteen or twenty the learner became a 'passed cleaner', allowed to fill temporary vacancies as a fireman until a permanent post became available. When registered as a fireman he could start to acquire the skills of the driver, and a similar path was trodden – from 'passed fireman' to emergency driver, then local freight and passenger driver, after which a select few would become main-line drivers. As Reynolds pointed out, much

In June 1889 Robert Roscoe was the subject of a brief biography in the 'Great Western Railway Magazine and Temperance Union Record'. Born in 1818, he 'entered the Service' (such was the military phraseology of the railways) in 1844. At that time he was one of only nine drivers working out of Paddington. Twice, though through no fault of his own, he was involved in collisions and came close to death. But his response was, 'I stuck to my engine'. When the article was written – by which time he had passed the age of seventy – he was at the peak of his profession, being driver of the Great Western's royal train.

The safety of the train depended much on the condition of the wheels and tyres, regularly checked by the wheel-tapper, who developed an ear for the sound 'ring'. This one, working for the Great Central Railway, was photographed in the 1890s.

Railways were still in their infancy when the 'London Saturday Journal' featured engine-drivers in a series of articles on 'Illustrations of Humanity' (below right). Though 'a new class of human beings', drivers were presented as 'on a level with drovers, driving cattle to market'. The writer therefore urged the companies to elevate as well as educate their drivers. Brunel, however, was one of many who argued in favour of illiterates, who, he believed, were more likely to pay close attention to their duties. Similarly he claimed that accidents would be invited by pampering the locomotive crew with a cab. Originally, driver and fireman were totally unprotected. In the 1840s the 'spectacle plate' or windscreen made its appearance, and from this the cab developed. Many enginemen were resistant to change, arguing that more enclosed cabs restricted their forward vision. The illustration from a late-nineteenth-century Christmas magazine (below left) looks very cosy but, in reality, the combination of draughts, damp and localised heat could be very punishing.

Henry Alken was a prolific painter and engraver of sporting and coaching subjects. In 1852, the year after his death, a set of four prints was published contrasting the drivers and guards of mail coaches and railway trains. While the railway driver was no match for the sartorial elegance of the stagecoach driver, the guard beats his predecessor hands down. This London & North Western guard (above left) might be mistaken for a member of a rifle regiment, and he cuts quite a dash. Passenger guards were more lavishly attired than goods guards, for the latter had little to do with the public. In 1849 a complete uniform for a passenger guard of the Bristol & Exeter Railway cost £5 1s 7d; for a goods guard it cost only £3 18s 0d. By the early twentieth century some of the former glory had passed. The London & North Western guard (above right) still has his patent leather belt and cartouche case, but his coat is shorter and his cap more utilitarian. (Photograph from Charles H. Grinling, 'The Ways of Our Railways', 1905.)

patience was required if this route to advancement was to be followed:

> If we were to sum up the conditions on which a man can command the regulator of an engine, it would read thus: Miles to run, 200,000; coals to break up and put into the fire-box in their proper place, 3000 tons; day work, 3 years; night work, 4 years; Sunday work, 25 days per year; innumerable hairbreadth escapes, eyes constantly on the roll, the mouth shut and the ears open, an iron constitution, a whistle in the lips, a warm heart, and an intelligent head, with the motto, 'Wait'.

Footplatemen worked long hours and main-line men could often find themselves far from home at the end of the day. When obliged to use company hostels on such occasions, drivers and firemen ate at separate tables and by the end of the nineteenth century, at Kentish Town (at least), public houses had separate bars for drivers and firemen.

Amongst railway workers as a whole, drivers were well paid, the rate depending on a man's particular grading. In 1852, for example, the London & North Western had 50 drivers of the fourth grade, earning 5s 6d a day; 40 drivers of the first class, earning 7s 6d; and 20 'special class' drivers, earning 8s 6d. In 1913 Kenney concluded that the average weekly wage of a driver working six days was 40s, although overtime and bonuses would bring this up to 45s 11d, or roughly 7s 8d a day.

Whether a train carried goods or passengers, responsibility for its safety rested with the guard. In the case of passenger trains, the importance of the guard was expressed in his uniform, which outdid all others in its splendour. F. S. Williams wrote: 'Proudly as Louis XIV in his royal robes, the British railway guard, standing in full uniform at the side of the winged express preparing to start, may lay his hand on his heart and say, "Le train, c'est moi."' The London & Birmingham Railway and its successor, the London & North Western, originally had two guards on main line passenger trains, the under guard riding in a van next to the tender, against which he turned his back so that his attention might be fixed on the train. As the company's

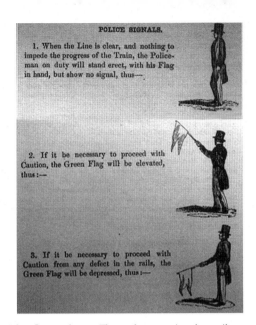

Originally, signals were given by hand, using either flags or lamps. The work was assigned to railway policemen, who continued to work the first fixed signals. Railway policemen were sworn in by a magistrate and wore uniforms which closely paralleled those of the regular police.

regulations stated, he should spend his time 'looking alternately down either side, and noting any irregularity in the running – any particular oscillation of a Carriage, or any signal which may be made by a Passenger'. Not until the Regulation of Railways Act, 1868, was it laid down that every train travelling more than twenty miles without stopping was to be provided with 'efficient means of communication between the passengers and the servants of the company in charge of the train', a requirement satisfied by the introduction of the communication cord. Old navy man that he was, Peter Lecount advised the London & Birmingham to appoint old seamen as guards: as well as being used to working in rough weather, they had a knowledge of knots and splicing that would be invaluable for securing luggage. He recommended that they be issued with wire spectacles to protect their eyes from smuts thrown out by the engine, as well as small telescopes in order to keep a better lookout.

Much of the guard's time, however, was devoted to record-keeping. In the 1880s, for example, the Midland Railway superintendent's office received 1600 record sheets (or 'journals') each day, on which guards had recorded details of their journeys tabulated in 44 columns. In addition to all of this, the guard was expected to mollify passengers and to keep an avuncular eye on any unaccompanied female passengers.

Safe working of the railway system depended on the skill and attentiveness of the signalman, but he was an individual rarely, if ever, encountered by members of the public. Station staff, guards and (on occasion) footplatemen all might supplement their wages by tips from the public (even though companies frowned on the practice), but, however much a signalman might give service beyond the call of duty, he was unable to benefit in this manner.

Originally, the task of signalling trains was assigned to railway policemen, hence the nickname 'bobbies' being given to signalmen as well as policemen in railwaymen's slang. There was a vast difference in the duties and responsibilities of signalmen in the early days, when trains were few and infrequent, compared with the latter part of the nineteenth century, when an enormous traffic had been built up. Similarly,

A busy signal cabin at Charing Cross (above left). Before the introduction of electrically operated equipment, working the signals involved much physical effort. The country signalman had things more easy, although his duties might, as in this case (above right), involve operating a level crossing. (Engravings from John Pendleton, 'Our Railways', published in 1894.)

there was a difference between the life of a country signalman and one who operated one of the principal boxes at a major junction. W. M. Ackworth described the main 'A' box at Waterloo in 1889. At busy times of the day, three trains arrived or departed every four minutes. A team of ten signalmen, working three shifts, operated the 209 levers in the box. Each man pulled a lever about every fifteen seconds. To the arduous physical labour involved was added the mental strain imposed by the heavy responsibility and the need for constant concentration. At a country box, the man might spend as much time tending his roses as his signalling equipment.

The passion for gardening was shared by many station staff and was encouraged by the railway companies as it encouraged pride in the upkeep of stations as well as being good for public relations. The North Eastern Railway set aside 200 guineas each year to be distributed to the best-kept stations, while the Great Western awarded a total of £250 in prize money, which would be granted only if the offices, waiting rooms and lavatories were equally spotless.

A picturesque rural halt or the station of a market town was very different from one of the major termini. Wanstrow, near Frome in Somerset, was the smallest station on the Great Western Railway, and it had no staff of its own. On winter days in the Edwardian era, when five trains a day in each direction stopped there, a platelayer would light the station-room fire and see to the lamps in the evening. Periodically, the station-master of nearby Witham was required to inspect the station's condition. Compare this with Nottingham, where F. S. Williams tells us in the early 1880s that 'there are some twenty clerks, twenty guards, thirty porters, forty-five signalmen, a dozen men and boys in connection with the parcel office, besides lamp-men, carriage-cleaners, ticket-examiners, shunters, fish-porters, and others, about 170 in all'; or Newcastle, where in 1901 the station-master had under him 11 assistant station-masters, 300 porters, 96 signalmen, 16 clerks, 22 booking clerks, and 34 parcels clerks; or Paddington, which had a staff of 720 in 1904–5.

The station-master was a man of some substance, especially at the larger stations, where he might possess a frock coat and silk hat for special occasions – a sure sign of his middle-class status. Joseph Pascoe wrote of the station-master in 1878: 'It would be difficult to state at what time of the day his duties commence, and at what time they are completed.' At any hour of the night he was likely to be woken from his sleep in order to deal with some emergency. The rules and regulations of the

The 'Break of Gauge' at Gloucester, where the standard-gauge railway from Birmingham met the broad gauge of the Great Western. 'You will hear the Railway Policeman bawling into the deaf Passenger's ear that he must dismount; you will see the anxious Mamma hastening her family in its transit from carriage to carriage, dreading the penalty of being too late; your dog will chance to have his foot crushed between wheelbarrows and porters' baskets – howling more terrifically than the engine itself. . . . The reality far surpasses the bustle of our illustration.' In fact, this engraving, from the 'Illustrated London News' of 6th June 1846, clearly exaggerates the horrors of transhipment.

London & North Western in 1849 included the following instructions for station-masters:

5. He is to take care that all the Servants at his Station come on duty clean in their persons and clothes, shaved, and with their shoes brushed.

6. He is also to cause the Station to be kept clear of weeds, and have the ballast raked and preserved in neat order. He must be careful that all stores supplied for the Station are prudently and economically used, and that there is no waste of gas, oil, coal, or stationery.

Stationery was consumed in enormous quantities, for railway companies were vast bureaucracies which thrived on paperwork – and much of it passed through the station-master's hands. The importance of record-keeping no doubt partly explains that, while some station-masters rose from the ranks of porters, most commonly they had started as booking clerks, gradually learning the working of all aspects of the station. Annual salaries varied enormously, generally ranging in the 1880s from around £95 to a maximum of about £350, perhaps with a house thrown in at a fixed rent of £20. There were perquisites, such as free travel, and so important was the question of status that a salary of between £120 and £130 might entitle a station-master to a first-class pass.

Porters, of whom there were some 50,000 in the late 1870s, were far from homogeneous. At a large station one might find both passenger and goods porters, office porters and letter porters, clock-room porters and cloakroom porters, and

In 1881 the London, Brighton & South Coast Railway took a series of photographs as a record of staff uniforms. There were subtle distinctions between each. Here, from the left, are shown: a van guard; carman; head porter; general porter; cloakroom porter; and station superintendent's clerk.

Until 1902 the Midland Railway station at Chedworth, in Gloucestershire, was a temporary building, part of which was a converted carriage. This photograph, c.1899, shows Freddie Tucker, the station-master, 'Curley' Beames, porter, and George Rook, platelayer. If Freddie Tucker had ambition, promotion would mean transfer to another station, with repeated moves if he were successful. A rural porter or platelayer, however, might well continue to live in the same cottage, doing the same job, all his working life.

Right: A ticket examiner sets the train indicator at Leicester station in the 1890s. Someone else probably had the responsibility of regulating the station clocks. The introduction of standardised time-keeping, and the move away from local time, was one of the great contributions of the railways.

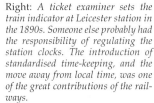

Left: The illustrator Richard Doyle (1824–83) drew this sketch of the Great Western booking office at Paddington in 1840. The booking clerk stands at an open desk and is filling out the ticket ('a piece of buff paper') by hand. It was in this year that Thomas Edmondson invented a machine capable of issuing standardised, pre-printed tickets. Without such a machine, chaos would have ensued as the number of journeys increased. For example, the 22 booking clerks at Newcastle Central station issued 3,159,480 tickets in 1899, an average of 8656 a day. By that date booking offices were well organised.

An office interior at the Euston headquarters of the London & North Western Railway. What clerical work lacked by way of remuneration was partly compensated for by respectability, security and the prospect of a pension. (Photograph from Charles H. Grinling, 'The Ways of Our Railways', 1905.)

With cash in his Gladstone bag, and with a well-built assistant to protect him as well as to carry the heavier account books, M. J. Widdowson, pay clerk on the London to Stafford section of the London & North Western Railway, does his rounds in the 1860s.

lamp porters. These last were responsible for all the oil lamps at a station, including those at the front and back of the train, and the interior lamps which were dropped in through the carriage roof. The job of cleaning, trimming and lighting the lamps was the province of 'lamp lads' or 'lampies' – fourteen-year-old boys who perhaps dreamed of rising to become station-master of a great terminus.

It was possible to rise from the ranks. At the beginning of the twentieth century at least five chairmen of railway companies had worked their way up, as had quite a number of general managers and other senior officials, with a top general manager commanding a salary as high as £5000 a year. But the number of such positions was small and, as Charles Grinling put it in 1905, 'For the vast majority railway employment means a steady and rather monotonous "grind", not at all magnificently remunerated; and not a few leave it to seek – but not always to find – their fortune in other spheres.'

Writing in 1878, Joseph Pascoe suggested: 'It is probable that there is no better clerk-school than railways for becoming accustomed to hard work, for attainment of rapidity in writing, and for a certain adeptness in simple calculations.' Junior clerks, he alleged, were paid quite liberally, 'but the majority of adult railway clerks are the worst paid and the hardest worked of any of their class.' Large numbers (even those with responsibilities as cashiers) were earning less than £100 a year. Discipline was strict. In 1875 a young man starting a clerkship at the Buchanan Street, Glasgow, station of the Caledonian Railway remarked: 'The first thing I learned there was that Presbyterian strictness was nothing compared to one brand of railway rigidity.' Hours were long; in the second half of the nineteenth century a clerk might work from 9 a.m. to 6 p.m., with a half-day off on Saturday. It is not surprising, therefore, that the organisation of clerical workers was led by the railway workers who formed the Railway Clerks' Association in 1897, the membership of which grew from under 10,000 by 1910 to 42,000 in 1915.

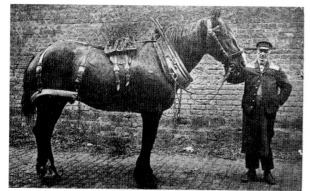

One of the oldest Great Western carmen and his horse, 1909 (left); and Great Eastern bay horse no. 2117 (better known, perhaps, as 'Bill'), with driver Cook (below). At this time the Great Western kept 600 horses in its Paddington stables alone. The Great Eastern owned 1750 horses in all, the bulk of them in London.

Railwaymen off the rails

Many railway workers were employed only indirectly with the running of trains, for railway companies provided other services to their customers. They put passengers up in their own hotels and fed them on their journey. They might carry them by ship. Their goods departments both collected and delivered loads of all kinds.

It is ironic that the railways, which many had prophesied would bring about the decline of the horse as a means of transport, should eventually have become amongst the largest operators of horse-drawn transport in Britain. In addition, they supported the equine activities of many private carriers and public transport undertakings. It has been said that without the services of horse-drawn vehicles railways would have been like stranded whales.

The horse departments of railway companies were significant undertakings. By the 1890s the Midland had the largest number of horses in London of any railway company. The stud of the London & North Western, on the other hand, was comparatively small. At about that time it employed 640 horses and about 2700 men in the metropolis, but this was because since its earliest days it put much of its carrying work out to contractors, including Pickford, which had an establishment equal to its own.

Some of the 113 staff at the Great Eastern stables at Hare Street, Bethnal Green, in 1911. The maintenance of fleets of road vehicles and the horses to pull them meant that amongst the ranks of 'railwaymen' were to be found horse-keepers as well as such craftsmen as saddlers, farriers and wheelwrights. (From 'Great Eastern Railway Magazine', May 1911.)

Towards the end of the nineteenth century competition for passengers prompted some railway companies to commence bus services to draw people to their stations. Such was the case in Pinner. The London & North Western opened a station at nearby Hatch End in 1842. In 1883 the Metropolitan Railway opened a station in the very heart of Pinner village. The London & North Western immediately started a bus service to its own station, and this ran until 1914. Throughout that time it had only one regular driver, George Bridge.

Shunting horses at the beginning of the twentieth century. These horses were the heaviest of all those employed by railway companies, and the work of the shunter himself was amongst the most dangerous.

The Great Western SS Ibex, which ferried passengers from Plymouth to Brest. Many 'railwaymen' were, in fact, merchant seamen. The Ibex was one of sixteen ships owned by the Great Western at this time. (From 'Great Western Railway Magazine', October 1909.)

Many of the horses used by railway companies started off on the farm. So, too, did many of the horsemen, for a countryman with a knowledge of horses could nearly always find a job with the railways. The politician Ernest Bevin was one of many who made that transition. Likewise, those living near the coast might find service in the maritime departments of railway companies. At the beginning of the twentieth century the London & South Western owned fifteen steamers, running to France and the Channel Islands. The Great Eastern had nine passenger and three cargo ships running between Harwich and the Continent. Several companies ran docks; the North Eastern Railway ranked amongst the largest dock owners of the United Kingdom.

The railway refreshment room sandwich entered early into catering folklore. In 1894 John Pendleton wrote:

> There is only three minutes in which to get your meal. You ask, in desperation, for a sandwich and a cup of coffee. The coffee is hot and nourishing. The sandwich is an overnight one. It has been in its glass prison for eight hours at least. The bread is stale, hard, and curled at the corners, and the ham looks the reverse of tempting.

Train and dining-car attendants of the London & North Western and Caledonian Railways (right), and hotel porters (with the head porter in the centre) of the Euston Hotel (above). (From Charles H. Grinling, 'The Ways of Our Railways', 1905.)

The uniform contractor to the Great Eastern Railway Hotels and Refreshment Department advertises in that company's magazine in October 1914 – by which time it was no doubt producing uniforms of a different, more military sort.

Railways were central to the development of both the modern restaurant and the modern hotel. The London & Birmingham was the first to provide hotel accommodation, opening two hotels at Euston in 1838–9. At first it tried to operate one of these itself but soon leased them both to a private hotelier, who went on to lease the first railway refreshment room at Wolverton in Buckinghamshire. The Great Western leased out its refreshment room at Swindon, the original 99-year lease of 1842 containing a clause obliging the company to stop all trains at Swindon for ten minutes. At first this was not onerous to the company, but as trains became faster and more frequent it became very irksome indeed, and in 1895 the lease was bought back for £100,000 – a full refund of the original capital. Refreshment rooms and trolleys, hotels and dining cars (introduced by the Great Northern Railway in 1879) offered much employment, the Midland Hotel at Manchester, for example, employing 380 people in 1904. Many of these workers were women.

A Midland Railway refreshment buffet stands outside the dining room of Derby station in 1908. Many companies ran their own bakeries to meet their needs.

A liftwoman of the London Electric Railway Company, photographed during the First World War, when fresh employment opportunities opened up for women.

Women railway workers

The census of 1851 listed 65,000 males in the category of 'Railway driver, etc., porter, etc., labourer, platelayer'. Of females in the same category it listed 54. Clearly, these workers fell into the *'et cetera'* groups! Nevertheless, throughout the Victorian and Edwardian periods many women did find employment on the railways, though not on the same scale as men, nor with the same visibility. Perhaps the only ones the public were likely to see were waitresses or barmaids at refreshment rooms and hotels. Many of these women, it seems, were the daughters or other relatives of railwaymen. Some concern was shown for the welfare of railway barmaids, who were seen to be in a vulnerable position. In the 1890s there was a Barmaids' Guild at Wolverton and a House of Rest, established by Lady Wolverton. By 1894 the barmaids of the Great Eastern's Liverpool Street station earned on average 10s a week (with

Women attendants at a railway refreshment room. In 1849 Francis Bond Head described the refreshment room at Wolverton, which at that time employed some sixteen women, including kitchen, scullery and laundry maids. Of the waitresses he wrote: 'The excellent matron . . . who has charge of these young people . . . with honest pride declares, that the breath of slander has never ventured to sully the reputation of any of those who have been committed to her charge.'

'no expenses except laundry bills') and were entitled to stay at a company hostel at Hackney Downs, 'where they are lodged and boarded, everything, even a piano and a housekeeper, being provided for their comfort and recreation'.

Most women worked behind the scenes, and many of them were engaged in tasks traditionally associated with women. Vast numbers of towels, tablecloths, sheets and antimacassars had to be washed each week, and many companies ran their own laundries, largely staffed by women. Some of the work they did with the needle was hard, for women also laboured at making and repairing the mountains of sacks that railways required. In the late 1880s, for example, the Midland had 450,000 sacks and employed twelve women to repair them.

The linen room in the Euston dining car depot of the London & North Western Railway (left), and the same company's laundry at Willesden, c.1905 (below). Even outside the home, women were largely restricted to 'women's work'.

By the end of the nineteenth century women were admitted in small numbers to the finishing and trimming shops of some railway carriage works. About a hundred were employed at Swindon in 1892 and were engaged in such activities as sewing, French-polishing and making the nets that went above seats to carry luggage. There was some concern over the place of women in such a male environment, and they were provided with a separate entrance and given different starting and leaving times.

workers, six of whom acted as bearers. A wreath was subscribed for by the station staff.

❖ ❖ ❖

MRS. CHARLOTTE HOSKINS who died on February 21st at the age of seventy-one years was employed in the Printing Department as a folder and book-sewer.

Having joined the service in 1864, Mrs. Hoskins had almost completed fifty years' service.

❖ ❖ ❖

MRS. C. HOSKINS.

Brief obituaries of employees are to be found in the staff magazines of railway companies. This one is taken from the 'Great Eastern Railway Magazine' of May 1913. The Great Eastern printing works at Stratford, in east London, employed over 100 men and women by the end of the 1880s, producing (amongst other things) the thousand or so forms which fed the bureaucracy.

Women workers polishing carriage panels in the workshops of the Great Eastern Railway at Stratford, where they also made window blinds and cushion cases. Women were first employed in 1894, and by 1911 (when this picture appeared in the 'Great Eastern Railway Magazine') some fifty or sixty girls worked there, the majority of them orphans of old railway workers.

Trainee women telegraph operators of the Great Western Railway in the early twentieth century. Women had been employed on this work almost from the birth of telegraphy, one story being that, around 1853, the chairman of the Electric & International Telegraph Company in London heard of the daughter of a railway station-master who had carried on all her father's telegraph work for three years, suggesting to him the possibility of training women telegraphists.

Railway work contributed but little to the four-hundred-fold increase in the numbers of women clerical workers that took place from 1861 to 1911. In that year there were 84,802 male railway clerks listed in the census, compared with only 1120 women. Not until January 1912 were the first 27 women clerks admitted to the Railway Clearing House, and all of them were relatives of male clerks. It was around 1875 that the London & North Western took on some women at Birmingham to undertake book-keeping in the goods department (where they received from 10s to 15s a week). Some kinds of office work were considered more suitable than others for women. In 1896, for example, Charles Booth reported that 'as typewriters [sic], copyists and telephone operators they are said to excel.' Typing was felt to resemble piano-playing. Women made good telegraphists and gained a foothold in that occupation well before the First World War opened up a range of new employment opportunities. At Edinburgh's Waverley station, for example, there were 40 female telegraphists in 1900, sending 4000 messages a day.

The welfare of railway workers

The railway companies used both the carrot and the stick in managing their staff. The stick was draconian discipline, exercised through the rule book, which every worker had to sign for on receipt. Breach of the rules could bring a fine or even dismissal. In 1873 the *Railway Service Gazette* carried a piece entitled 'The Railwayman's Ten Commandments', which included such injunctions as 'Honour thy official and carry tales' and 'Thou shalt commit 300 rules to memory'. The number and detail of the rules and regulations could be counterproductive, for workers in dispute with their employers could always 'work to rule', although the 1909 rule book of the Great Eastern's Stratford works even cautioned employees against 'not cheerfully . . . carrying out instructions'.

The carrot was the provision of cheap coal, free clothing, company housing, relative security, and the prospect of a pension. Charles Grinling wrote in 1905: 'For permanency, railway service in the United Kingdom is practically as good as the service of the Government.' The larger companies had their own superannuation schemes, while the smaller ones were able to participate in a superannuation fund run by the Railway Clearing House.

The companies' record in the case of accidents to their staff was less praiseworthy and they proved remarkably resistant to changing working practices that would have held back the tide of injury. Railway work was the third most dangerous occupation. In 1876, for example, Board of Trade figures (which probably underestimate) showed that 1 in 416 railway servants was killed, and 1 in 86

Railway companies were responsible for the provision of much housing for their workers, especially in such towns as Wolverton, Derby and Swindon. This was often of a higher standard than that which most workmen might expect. These cottages (top) were built by the Great Western Railway in Faringdon Street, Swindon, in 1846–7. The 1851 census indicates that many of them were occupied by foremen at the nearby works. The rear alley between the cottages of Exeter Street and those of Taunton Street (bottom) shows the external privies, converted into stores when the buildings were refurbished in the 1970s.

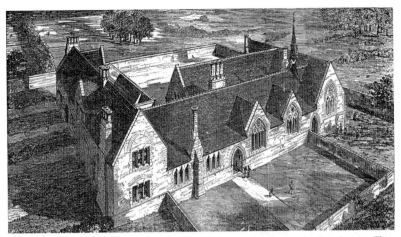

In railway towns the company often provided churches and schools as well as houses. The new school at Stantonbury, shown in this engraving from the 'Illustrated London News' of 19th June 1858, was built by the London & North Western Railway to take one hundred boys and one hundred girls, mainly the children of their workers at nearby Wolverton.

injured. Between 1872 and 1876 nearly 3000 railway workers are reckoned to have lost their lives. Shunting – the coupling and uncoupling of carriages or wagons in order to sort them into trains – was particularly dangerous, figures for 1912 showing that one in ten shunters was either killed or injured. Workmen's compensation was slow to come. Most companies accepted responsibility for payment under an Act of 1880, but it was not until 1897 that they could be compelled to do so. The position before 1880 was summed up by a goods guard of the Taff Vale Railway. When asked by a royal commission what compensation was paid by the company to widows, he replied, 'I believe the compensation they receive is a nice coffin'.

Many accidents resulted from the long hours that men were expected to work. An attempt was made in 1877 to limit working hours, but the provisions of the Bill which was introduced applied only to railwaymen actually engaged in working the traffic, for the real concern was to protect the passengers rather than the workers.

Both heavy drinking and total abstinence were strong amongst railwaymen. The Great Western Railway Coffee Tavern Company Ltd had a capital of between £5000 and £6000 and was set up in 1885 to provide non-alcoholic refreshment for railway workers. The tavern shown here was at St David's station, Exeter, and was opened in 1890.

The Percy Main North Eastern Railway Workmen's Silver Prize Band, photographed in 1911. The band, which was formed around 1899, originated in the mutual improvement class of the Locomotive Department and included engine-drivers, firemen, fitters and joiners amongst its members.

But the 'railway interest' was strongly represented in Parliament, and the Bill was thrown out. It was not for another ten years that the Board of Trade started to collect data systematically on the hours worked by railwaymen and even then it only required information from the companies if there had been a train accident. Personal accidents, such as those befalling a shunter, were excluded. In 1891 a Select Committee on Railway Servants (Hours of Labour) was established. Amongst the evidence was that relating to the death of 59-year-old John Gurr, who was killed while fog-signalling on the Brighton line in 1888. At the time of his death he had been on duty, in the fog and freezing cold, for $23^1/2$ hours out of the previous 30. John Choules of the Midland & South West Junction Railway had worked on 24 of the 27 days preceding his death in a shunting accident, working on average 12 hours and 58 minutes a day. The Select Committee (of which nearly a third of the members were railway directors) made weak proposals which led to a mouse of an Act in 1893 and the men's demand for a maximum eight-hour day was not met before the First World War.

A strong labour organisation might have improved the men's position, but a number of factors militated against its development. The considerable number of grades in the industry made unity difficult and the attitude of the companies, which was both paternalistic and dictatorial, militated against effective organisation. The Amalgamated Society of Railway Servants had been formed in 1871, but the membership of over 17,000 in 1872 had fallen to 6300 ten years later. None of the railway companies was willing to recognise it as a bargaining agent, and it had none of the strength and status of the great amalgamated societies on which it was modelled. In 1913 the ASRS amalgamated with two other unions to form the National Union of Railwaymen. Between 1913 and 1915 a 'Triple Alliance' was formed between the railwaymen, the miners and the transport workers – but it was not to show its teeth until after the First World War.

Further reading

A whole library could be filled with books on the railways of Britain, many containing valuable information on the lives of railway workers. An essential guide to the literature is:

Ottley, George. *Bibliography of British Railway History*. George Allen & Unwin, 1966. Supplements, HMSO, 1988, and National Railway Museum, 1998.

The following books have been found particularly useful:

Ackworth, W. M. *The Railways of England*. John Murray, 1889.
Bagwell, Philip. *The Railwaymen*. George Allen & Unwin, 1963.
Brooke, David. *The Railway Navvy*. David & Charles, 1983.
Burton, Anthony. *The Railway Builders*. John Murray, 1992.
Cattell, John, and Falconer, Keith. *Swindon: The Legacy of a Railway Town*. HMSO, 1995.
Coleman, Terry. *The Navvies*. Hutchinson, 1965.
Conder, F.R. *Personal Recollections of English Engineers*, 1868. Reprinted as *The Men Who Built Railways*, with an introduction by Jack Simmons; Thomas Telford, 1983.
Grinling, Charles H. *The Ways of Our Railways*. Ward, Lock, 1905.
Hawkings, David. *Railway Ancestors*. Alan Sutton/Public Record Office, 1995.
Hudson, Kenneth. *Working to Rule*. Adams & Dart, 1970.
Kenney, Rowland. *Men and Rails*. T. Fisher Unwin, 1913.
McKenna, Frank. *The Railway Workers 1840–1970*. Faber & Faber, 1980.
Pascoe, Joseph. *Our Railways*. C. Kegan Paul, 1878.
Pendleton, John. *Our Railways*. Cassell, 1894.
Reynolds, Michael. *Engine-Driving Life*. Crosby Lockwood, 1881.
Richards, Jeffrey, and MacKenzie, John M. *The Railway Station*. Oxford University Press, 1986.
Richards, Tom. *Was Your Grandfather a Railwayman?* Federation of Family History Societies, 1995.
Thomas, David St John. *The Country Railway*. David St John Thomas, 1991.
Williams, Alfred. *Life in a Railway Factory*. First published 1915. Reprinted with an introduction by Michael Justin Davis; Alan Sutton, 1986.
Williams, F.S. *Our Iron Roads*. Third edition, 1883. Reprinted by Gresham, 1981.

Places to visit

There are many preserved steam railways which give the flavour of railway work and life. Three published guides to these are:

Cockman, F.G. *Discovering Preserved Railways*. Shire, fifth edition 1997.
Lambert, Anthony J. *Enjoy Britain: Steam Railways*. AA Publishing, 1998.
Ross, Mike (editor). *Still Steaming: The Guide to Britain's Steam Railways, 1999–2000*. Marksman, 1999.

On the Internet, a listing of railway museums and preserved railways will be found at: www.ukhrail.uel.uk/abc.html

Of the many railway museums, two can be specially recommended:

National Railway Museum, Leeman Road, York YO26 4XJ. Telephone: 01904 621261. Website: www.nrm.org.uk
Steam: Museum of the Great Western Railway, Kemble Drive, Swindon, Wiltshire SN2 2TA. Telephone: 01793 466646. Website: www.swindonweb.com/steam

North Eastern Railway police officers at Hull docks with their dogs. This photograph was taken in 1912, five years after the company claimed to have been the first to introduce dogs for detective work and to increase the security of goods in transit. (From the 'North Eastern Railway Magazine'.)